Treat Yo

T0359477

Treat Your Chronic Fatigue Syndrome Yourself

Jon Gamble

BA ND Adv Dip Hom

Series Editor: Nyema Hermiston
Karuna Publishing
2021

©Jon Gamble 2021

Published by
Karuna Publishing
21 Hambridge Road
Yerrinbool NSW 2575
Australia

All correspondence to the above address or by email to:
enquiries@karunapublishing.com.au

*This book is not intended to replace competent medical advice, nor is
self-diagnosis recommended in the absence of adequate evaluation by
a health professional. In all cases, please seek the advice of a medical
professional, and advise him or her of any treatment you are undergoing.
The author is a health professional in private practice. The therapeutic
recommendations in this book are provided only as examples of successful
treatments that have been used with patients. The suggestions in this book
are not suitable for patients with severe allergies that cause anaphylactic
reactions.*

ISBN: 978-0-6484144-4-5

CONTENTS

INTRODUCTION

When I first started in clinical practice in 1987, Chronic Fatigue Syndrome, or 'CFS' was virtually unknown and patients suffering were often called 'malingerers'. In those days, it was more often called 'ME' or Myalgic Encephalomyelitis, the title indicating the standout symptoms of profound fatigue, sleep abnormalities, pain and other symptoms made worse by exertion. Ironically, the very first patient to walk into my newly opened clinic was a woman in her 30s, suffering from a range of severe symptoms I now recognise was Chronic Fatigue Syndrome. I was a rookie, straight out of college, and not really sure what I was doing, or more to the point, what exactly it was that I was treating. I gave her a number of medicines, but little helped her. I didn't then understand the multiple pathologies which I have since seen, that lie beneath CFS.

Imagine my surprise when thirty years later, this woman, now in her 60s, walked back into my clinic, with the same, but now more chronic symptoms. She had of course tried many different treatments over those years. She had heard about a test that I was using on CFS patients that she thought might help her. This time, I could see exactly what it was that was fuelling her symptoms. Due to this understanding, I was able to target her treatment at its cause. Now, she is almost completely better. Her illness was prolonged not because it was difficult to treat, but because the cause of her illness went unrecognised by many practitioners, including myself.

Since that time, an increasing number of patients with CFS began coming into my practice. Gradually, patient by patient, through trial and error, I managed to develop an understanding of the nature and causes of CFS, which made treatment much more straightforward. I have used a wide range of therapies, and am happy to report that some of them are surprisingly effective.

I came to see that most long-term CFS patients have a collection of different conditions, which coalesce to form this syndrome. While symptoms differ in each patient, some of the causes are common. Understanding these causes in each individual, is the key to unlocking the CFS puzzle. What I am offering here to readers, is an overview of what I have learned about treating CFS over 30 years.

By calling this book 'Treat Your CFS Yourself' I am suggesting you use the information here not to treat this complex condition yourself, but to initiate some helpful interventions, and orchestrate your own treatment plan with your health professional, to shorten your period of suffering.

I hope the information in this booklet helps you or a loved one to find a solution for this debilitating and 'untreatable' condition.

Jon Gamble

PART ONE

CFS OVERVIEW

I
Chronic Problems For Chronic Fatigue Sufferers

- Being Believed
- Getting a Diagnosis
- The Devil in the Detail

Being Believed

Some patients wonder, 'Is this all in my head?' If your leg was in plaster and you were hobbling around on crutches, your suffering could be seen. With CFS, your suffering is invisible, because no one can 'see' your symptoms. Add to that, your pathology tests are all normal. Your doctors and loved ones start to doubt you. It may have been hinted that you're a malingerer. Even worse, you may have been told 'it's all in your head' and you are referred to a psychologist. Your doctor may offer you antidepressant medication. Don't worry, this is common! By this point, it's easy for people with CFS to start doubting their own symptoms and their own judgement, because of the number of people who think that maybe they just need psychological help.

Having established what CFS is *not*, the real issue is: what is CFS? The answer to this is both simple and complex. First the simple answer. Like all syndromes, CFS may have a single cause, but often it results from a range of different causes, sometimes unrelated, which over time, have combined to form a *collection of symptoms* that you experience as CFS. The key to successful treatment, is to know what the components or causes of your CFS are. Finding these causes when your pathology results are all normal is crucial. Fortunately, specialised tests have become available to help explain CFS symptoms and provide an individualised treatment path.

Getting a Diagnosis

There is no definitive test to diagnose CFS, so after a raft of medical tests, a CFS diagnosis is made by excluding other more serious illnesses. While this is a lot to go through, it is some relief to discover that you do not have a life-threatening illness.

While chronic tiredness is a key indicator of CFS, tiredness alone should not be diagnosed as CFS.

These conditions which cause fatigue are not CFS and must be properly investigated:

- Anaemia
- Depression
- Diabetes
- Malnutrition
- Sleep apnoea
- Thyroid disorders.

The following symptoms must be properly medically investigated:

- Fever (intermittent)
- Neurological symptoms

- Pain in localised areas
- Unexplained pains at night
- Weight loss.

!Before reading further, please ensure that you have had thorough medical examination and testing. If you've shown up all clear on your standard tests, and been given a diagnosis of CFS by your doctor, then read on!

The Devil in the Detail

In most cases, the cause or causes of your CFS can be found by studying your health history in great detail; that is the **timeline of your health since birth.** When did symptoms start? What happened at that time? Did an animal or insect ever bite you? What medications have you had? What injuries have you had? What was your physical and living environment like when you got sick? Were you really unwell that year after you had the flu? Did you get travellers' diarrhoea on an overseas trip? Have you been an avid bushwalker, etc.

II
SYMPTOMS OF CHRONIC FATIGUE SYNDROME

For a diagnosis of Chronic Fatigue Syndrome (CFS) to be made, you must have these symptoms:

- Your ability to function as you did before your symptoms started, is greatly reduced
- You have consistently experienced over the previous six months extreme fatigue not improved by rest (unrefreshing sleep)
- Post-exertion malaise.

Plus one of these symptoms:

- Chronic headaches or migraine
- Cold intolerance
- Dizziness
- Fibromyalgia (ongoing muscle pain)
- Impaired memory and concentration
- Insomnia
- Joint pain
- Low blood pressure (dizziness) after lying down
- Muscle weakness
- Ongoing sore throat and tender lymph nodes.

Associated conditions may be:

- Chemical sensitivities
- Food intolerances
- Irritable Bowel Syndrome
- Irritable Bladder Syndrome
- Restless Leg Syndrome.

III
Fibromyalgia

Although fibromyalgia is a syndrome in itself, generalised muscle pain diagnosed as fibromyalgia, is often a component of CFS. Fibromyalgia can be caused by chronic bacterial or viral infection, and requires appropriate testing.

Tick borne illnesses such as Lyme Disease can also result in fibromyalgia.

Symptoms include:

- Generalised muscle pain in all limbs with tender, or 'trigger' points
- Tingling or prickling sensation in muscles when pressure is applied
- Skin sensitivity
- Temporomandibular joint dysfunction (jaw pain).

See Chapter 8: Fibromyalgia

IV

Is CFS 'Real' or Is It All In My Mind?

A problem arises when a single title is used to describe complex syndromes. It has become clear that most CFS is more than one illness and can have a variety of different causes. Stress does make CFS worse and can be the cause of symptoms such as depression, but there is usually an underlying cause in addition to stress. Having CFS is a stress in itself!

Many CFS patients have doubted their own perceptions and the reality of their disease because of the sceptical attitudes of their health practitioners, family or friends. If conventional medical tests fail to return evidence of abnormal pathology, some practitioners dismiss their patient as 'hysterical'.

I have found that CFS patients are certainly not hysterical and their illness is real. If patients with chronic disease weren't anxious and depressed before their illness was dismissed as "all in their head" they can soon become depressed or anxious after receiving this news. Once CFS has been identified and treated, their emotional state improves. That is to say you may have anxiety or depression as a reaction to your CFS, or your CFS may have appeared during a time of high stress, but generally CFS is a separate entity from anxiety and/or depression.

There *are* reasons why you have CFS. It's not all in your head. There *is* an answer and it may be closer than you think. Where possible, try doing some activity that you can manage and that you really enjoy. There is an array of meditation Apps available. One of them is bound to suit you. Meditation can be surprisingly helpful to stay positive and keep a sense of yourself.

See Chapter 12: Trauma.

V
Tests

No single test can confirm a diagnosis of CFS. If standard medical testing doesn't shed any light on your problem, other tests are available from some health professionals. Targeted, specialised pathology tests based on your individual need, are needed to identify where the problem(s) lie.

However, it's a really big ocean out there. It cannot be overemphasised that it is the medical timeline in the first consultation that shows you where the best place is to go fishing. Fishing in the wrong place means you find nothing. This can be demoralising for patient and practitioner, not to mention expensive, as functional pathology tests can be costly.

Testing may include:

* Comprehensive Digestive Stool Analysis
* Complete Microbiome Stool Test
* Food Sensitivity Test (IgG, IgA)
* Specialised blood tests, eg testing for Lyme disease

- Tissue Mineral Analysis (*Oligoscan*[1], Hair Tissue Mineral Analysis)
- Organic Acid Test (OAT) for individual metabolic profiles to identify:

  - Chemical agents
  - Herbicide residues
  - Infective agents

- Super-specialised pathology tests to identify mould biotoxins and endocrine–disrupting chemicals.

---

[1] See Appendix C: *Oligoscan*

VI
Causes and Treatment Overview

Because CFS can be complex to treat, it is best managed with an experienced health professional and/or an integrative medicine doctor. Detailed information about your health timeline is crucial. If you can't remember some details, ask a family member. *Make sure your health professional knows these details.*

The treatment guidelines outlined in **Part 2** of this booklet are designed for CFS sufferers to get on a more supportive track and offer some relief of symptoms. **But it is tough** if you are dealing with this condition alone. To fully recover from CFS, the majority of people need the help of a competent health professional. Find a practitioner who listens to you, understands you, and shows a keen interest to help you find a solution. If you feel like you are being brushed off, change practitioners. The practitioner could be out of his or her depth.

Ideally, your practitioner will:

• Take a detailed medical history
• Conduct a physical examination if appropriate
• Carefully assess all of your symptoms
• Order appropriate specialised tests

- Be able to explain to you why you have your symptoms
- Clearly outline your overall treatment to you.

Treatment plans should be:
- Based on the verified causes of your CFS
- Be an individually tailored solution for you, rather than a generic product.

Features of a comprehensive treatment plan:
- Dietary recommendations
- Nutritional supplements
- Herbal or homeopathic medicines
- Detoxification methods
- Other individualised therapies.

Length of Treatment

While some forms of CFS respond more quickly than others, generally, treatment is a long-term process. If your CFS has developed in the past 12 months and it follows a viral illness like influenza or glandular fever, and you were previously healthy, the treatment period may be relatively short.

Far more commonly though, CFS treatment is a step by step process over time, due to its multiple causes. Factors that prolong the treatment time are the length of time you have suffered from CFS and the number of different causes which make up your symptom picture.

Sensitivity

CFS sufferers are generally more sensitive to their external environment than the general population. This concept can be difficult to convey to others. Again, there is nothing external to see. This sensitivity can translate into needing smaller doses of prescribed medicines, herbs and other products. Perfumes, pollens, WiFi and mobile phones can make you feel worse. Some people cannot even enter my office unless we switch off the WiFi. It makes them feel on edge, almost like the ground is trembling.

If you have these sensitivities, take heart that you are not alone and you are not going crazy. You have a hyper-reactive nervous system. This oversensitivity sometimes limits the range of treatments that can be applied to you. Fortunately, homeopathic medicines are gentle enough for hypersensitive patients to tolerate. They can be prepared to suit each person to avoid sensitivity reactions and enable positive responses.

PART TWO

THE MULTIPLE CAUSES OF CFS AND HOW TO NAVIGATE YOUR TREATMENT

Important note:

Treatment recommendations in this section are intended for readers to gain an understanding of what the cause of their CFS might be, and to begin using simple strategies which may offer some relief of symptoms. Ultimately, effective treatment requires the engagement of a health professional who has experience with and an understanding of CFS. It can be helpful for patients to inform themselves about CFS and form a partnership with their practitioner to guide their own treatment plan.

CHAPTER 1

POST-VIRAL FATIGUE

Post-viral chronic fatigue in a previously healthy person is the most simple form of CFS. Common viruses causing this type of CFS are the *Epstein Barr Virus* (EBV), *Cytomegalovirus* and more recently, Covid19 coronavirus.

EBV (Infectious mononucleosis) causes what we know as Glandular Fever, also commonly known as 'the kissing disease' due to its easy spread amongst teenagers and students. While *Cytomegalovirus* is different from EBV, its symptoms are very similar to Glandular Fever symptoms. Sometimes, the viral episode is subtle, and the sufferer is unaware they have caught a virus, and experience a period of ongoing fatigue.

Initial symptoms:

- Body pain
- Fatigue
- Night sweats
- Recurring fever
- Recurring sore throat
- Swollen glands - neck, armpits, groin.

Once the viral event has passed, recovery is usually slow.

Post-viral CFS can occur at any age, but most commonly occurs in the 13 - 30 year age group.

Any viral illness can result in poor energy and slow recovery. As well as glandular fever, the 'flu or a case of shingles (*Herpes Zoster*) can be the trigger. Sometimes, the exact virus is difficult to identify.

More recently, significant numbers of people recovering from Covid19 are reporting prolonged recovery times with ongoing debilitating fatigue.

Even if it was experienced many years before, a common statement made by CFS sufferers is: "I have never been fully well since I had that virus". When the 'virus' has been more subtle, the patient does not always recall having had a significant viral event before their CFS symptoms began. The most frequent comment from patients is: "Every few weeks it feels like I have a sore throat coming on, but it never amounts to much. I just get more fatigue".

More chronic symptoms are:

- Difficult concentration
- Foggy head
- Muscle pain after exertion
- Recurring fevers
- Recurring sore throats.

Treatment

Post-viral CFS is usually the most responsive to treatment and can often be resolved within two months. Therapeutic approaches for fatigue after any virus follow a similar theme, although differences in presenting symptoms require individualised treatment.

Immune support using nutrients and herbal medicines in post-viral chronic fatigue are important. Some have direct antiviral effects on the body and are well understood to be important for normal immune function. They are available from many outlets. Follow the recommended dosages on the containers.

Nutrients:

- Zinc – up to 50 mg per day
- Vitamin C – up to 4000 mg per day
- Vitamin D – up to 5000 iu per day.

Herbal medicines:

- Andrographis
- Astragalus
- Echinacea
- Olive leaf extract.

I have found that an individually prescribed homeopathic medicine offers the most rapid and effective resolution of post viral chronic fatigue.

CHAPTER 2

GUT INFECTIONS

Since the 1970s, the human gut flora has been negatively impacted by the increasing use of broad–spectrum antibiotics to treat infection, and the wide use of antibiotics in agriculture.

Repeated courses of antibiotics prescribed for infections can cause a syndrome called gut dysbiosis, (disordered gut bacteria), particularly in young children. This is caused by the population of beneficial gut bacteria decreasing and an increase and overpopulation of other organisms which disrupt normal gut function, such as bacterial pathogens and yeasts such as *Candida albicans*.

The term *gut dysbiosis* describes any imbalance in the gut flora. Contributing factors to gut dysbiosis are poor diet, with an excess of convenience foods, sugary foods and too few wholefoods like fruit, vegetables, whole grains, and quality proteins. Chlorinated drinking water, while purifying the water, may also impact on the gut microbiome, by affecting the good bacteria.

When out of balance, a range of different organisms can cause gut dysbiosis which can lead to Irritable Bowel Syndrome (IBS) which also needs to be treated. It is common for people with CFS to also have IBS.

Left untreated, gut dysbiosis can lead to an inflammatory effect on the bowel wall, causing it to become permeable to minute food particles (leaky gut) and cause food sensitivities.

Causative factors of gut dysbiosis:

- Chemical exposure, eg glyphosate
- Chronic diarrhoea
- Poor diet
- Repeated antibiotic therapy
- Oral Contraceptive Pill.

Gut dysbiosis affects the whole body leading to these symptoms:

- Aggravation after sugary foods
- Fatigue
- Foggy thinking, aggravated by some foods
- Mood swings, aggravated by some foods
- Oral, vaginal or rectal thrush
- Sugar cravings
- 'Wired' anxious feeling in the body.

Another gut dysbiosis is bacterial overgrowth in the small intestine, known as 'Small Intestine Bacterial Overgrowth' (SIBO), where unwanted bacteria become too plentiful, due to low numbers of beneficial bacteria.

Common bacteria causing SIBO symptoms are:

- Klebsiella
- Citrobacter
- Streptoccocus
- Clostridia

To be clear: these bacteria are *normal* micro-residents of the gut, but have opportunistically over-colonised the small intestine, for these reasons:

- Beneficial bacteria have become denuded, through poor diet; starchy, sweet foods like white bread, white flour products, buns, cakes, and other sugary foods.

- Over time, multiple courses of antibiotics have destroyed too much beneficial gut bacteria, so the residents of the large intestine have moved into the small intestine and overgrown there.
- It is the gut which most commonly bears the brunt of stress, and long-term stress has been shown to negatively affect the gut flora. People literally say: "That really kicked me in the guts,""I have a gut feeling about this," "It's a pain in the arse" etc.

SIBO Symptoms:
- Bloating
- Constipation
- Diarrhoea
- Flatulence
- Nausea
- Sugar cravings
- Abdominal cramping.

Severe, longstanding SIBO can also lead to 'Leaky Gut Syndrome'. Due to constant low-grade inflammation caused by the overgrowth, the bowel wall becomes more permeable, allowing minute particles of food to pass through the gut wall and into the bloodstream, rather than being completely digested.

When you have leaky gut, you experience other general symptoms as well as gut symptoms. These symptoms usually occur after eating sugar and starchy carbohydrates, sometimes even fruit. The bacteria need these foods to survive. This may be the reason why affected people have sugar and carbohydrate cravings.

Additional symptoms:

- Dizziness
- Headache
- Joint pain
- Mood swings
- Poor concentration
- Symptoms that are difficult to explain.

If you have these symptoms, make sure to choose a health professional who recognises this condition.

Tests

When usual measures are not effective, a stool analysis and/or gut microbiome test is needed to identify stubborn unwanted gut organisms so specific treatment can be given.

These are:

- Complete Digestive Stool Analysis
- Complete Gut Microbiome

(Both these tests show the functional contents of your gut. Lab specialists can determine the type of dysbiosis, and show the causes of leaky gut syndrome).

- Gut Permeability test — a urine test which detects the degree of permeability of your gut wall.
- SIBO Breath test - The gold standard test for diagnosing SIBO.

Treatment

The most important treatment for dysbiosis is to remove all sugars and refined carbohydrates from the diet for at least *eight weeks.* ***This can be challenging,*** because withdrawing sugary foods from your diet can lead to severe cravings for those foods. *Candida* organisms need sugars from sweet foods to survive. These are physical (not mental) cravings for sugary foods. The strength of your sugar craving indicates the seriousness of your *Candida* problem, which, once you recognise it, is easy to self-diagnose. **There is no other treatment option. Unless you avoid all refined starches and sugars, you will not get better.**

Sugars and refined carbohydrates include soft drinks, fruit juices, cakes, white bread, white pasta, white rice, sweet biscuits, beer, and dried fruit. Once you gain the understanding that your appetite is being dictated by sugar-loving *Candida*, which is the cause of your sugar cravings, it will help you to achieve a sugar free diet.

It is not usually necessary to withdraw yeast from your diet, (although you may have been asked to do so by your health professional). I find that yeast does not impede improvement if all dietary sugars are removed.

Unrefined, unprocessed (whole) grains are:

- Wholemeal pasta
- Brown rice
- Wholemeal crackers
- 100% wholemeal bread.

You do need to check labels. Many breads are labelled wholemeal, but may have as little as 20 per cent wholemeal flour in them. For example, 'Bread making flour' on labels = white flour.

Golden Rules for Treating Yeast (or Bacterial) Overgrowth

- Avoid all sugary food, white flour products, commercial breakfast cereals, soft drinks, dried fruit, honey and rice malt for at least eight weeks. (Stevia powder and Xylitol are safe, natural sweeteners to use.) Avoid the well-known artificial sweeteners.

- Eat small amounts of healthy foods every two to three hours.

- 100 per cent whole grains; wholemeal bread, brown rice, wholemeal pasta BUT only small portions and always with protein.

- Have protein with every snack or meal.

- Fresh fruit is usually fine during these eight weeks, but should be kept to a minimum, and only with protein. An example is apple with cheese.

- The FODMAPS[2] diet helps this type of gut issue.

If you experience hunger with weakness and dizziness between meals, it is most likely a low blood sugar (hypoglycaemic) reaction. This is remedied by eating a

---

[2] https://www.monashfodmap.com

protein-based snack every two hours throughout the day and having a similar snack at bedtime.

Protein foods are:

- Beef, lamb and pork
- Cheese
- Chicken
- Eggs
- Fish – fresh, or tinned (sardines, mackerel and salmon)
- Legumes (peas, beans and lentils); dips like hummus are a good way to have legumes
- Nuts
- Unsweetened yoghurt — add fresh fruit if desired.

Protein-based snacks examples:

- Hummus or bean dip with carrot and celery sticks
- Caesar salad — (ask for the egg on top)
- Wholemeal crackers, cheese and fruit
- Green salad and fish with brown rice or wholemeal bread
- Chicken and salad sandwich (100% wholemeal bread)
- Tub of plain, unsweetened yoghurt with a small amount of fresh fruit.

Because product names can be misleading, carefully read the labels to make sure you are getting 100 per cent wholemeal products. Buying from a health food or organic store helps you to become familiar with real 100 per cent wholegrain products. The extra cost means extra nutrition, particularly in B vitamins and fibre. This can be more economical than you may think, as whole grains are more satisfying, so you need smaller quantities of them.

Medicines:

To reduce both yeast and bacteria overgrowth in the gut:

Herbs

- Oregano Oil
- Clove Oil
- Thyme Oil
- Peppermint Oil
- Garlic
- Berberine, from barberry, or phellodendron

Nutritional Supplement

L-Glutamine powder is the main supplement that helps to heal the gut wall. When combined with Slippery Elm powder, better results are achieved.

Probiotics

Invariably, probiotics are an integral part of treatment. Once the unwanted bacteria and yeasts are reduced, it is time to take broad-spectrum probiotics, especially *Lactobacillus rhamnosus*. It is important to know specifically which probiotics you need, and not leave it to guesswork, as you may be feeding unwanted bacteria and starving out much-needed bacteria.

There are literally hundreds of costly probiotic products on the market. Homemade probiotics can be equally, if not more effective than commercial brands.

See Appendix A: Homemade Probiotics.

CHAPTER 3

THYROID DISORDERS

Thyroid dysfunction, especially hypothyroidism, is often one factor in the many causes of CFS. While thyroid disturbance is not the cause of CFS, it may be a part of your CFS picture. Undiagnosed and untreated hypothyroidism is an obstacle to the successful treatment of CFS.

Thyroid testing and treatment does need to be managed by a health professional. The main thyroid test ordered by your doctor is the 'TSH' (Thyroid Stimulating Hormone) test. Oftentimes, hypothyroid symptoms develop before they appear in blood test results. When test results are in normal range, many people still have symptoms of an under functioning thyroid, yet are told their thyroid function is normal.

Therefore, it is easy to discount the idea of having low thyroid function, because of a normal blood test result.

If this is your experience, and there are thyroid problems in your family, you may recognise these symptoms:

- Brain fog
- Bulging eyes
- Fatigue unexplained
- Hair loss
- Muscle pain
- Outer eyebrow loss
- Palpitations
- Tremor
- Weight gain
- Lump feeling in the throat impeding swallowing.

If you have some of these symptoms, you can ask your doctor for a full thyroid panel blood test: Free Triiodothyronine (FT3) and Free Thyroxine (FT4) plus Thyroid Antibodies. This extra information will enable your doctor to diagnose any hypothyroidism, autoimmune thyroiditis, or Hashimoto's Thyroiditis.

Some doctors also check muscle reflexes to see if they are slower than normal, to identify low thyroid function.

Additionally, ask your health professional to check your levels of these nutrients, which are essential for normal thyroid function:

- Iodine
- Selenium
- Zinc
- Vitamins B9 and B12.

Treatment

When thyroid dysfunction is fully addressed, patients notice a big difference in the way they feel.

Normal thyroid function depends on adequate levels of:

- Iodine
- Selenium
- Zinc
- B vitamins, especially B9 and B12

These supplements are also essential for good health in general. It is safe to take these supplements yourself, with the exception of iodine, which must be prescribed and monitored by a health professional.

Hashimoto's Thyroiditis can respond very well to a gluten-free diet. Details of gluten-free diets are abundant on websites, particularly the Coeliac Disease sites. A gluten sensitivity does not mean that you have Coeliac Disease. Or, if you have tested negative for Coeliac Disease, you may still have gluten sensitivity, which may be fuelling your auto-immune reaction in Hashimoto's Thyroiditis.

Hypothyroid supporting herbs are:

- Goji berries
- Rhodiola
- Siberian Ginseng
- Withania

These are available in retail outlets, but it is highly recommended to see a qualified health professional for your thyroid problems.

If you have been prescribed daily doses of thyroid hormone and it is not helping you, then the above nutrients and herbs may be more helpful. At this point you can decide if you would like to continue taking your medication, or try a dietary and nutritional approach, and seek wholistic treatment from an integrative doctor.

CHAPTER 4

BACTERIAL INFECTION

When you have ongoing symptoms that are unresponsive to treatments over a long period of time, an undetected infection could lie at the seat of your CFS. Low-grade chronic infections don't always show up on routine blood tests, so this is worth considering.

Some chronic bacterial infections are:

- *Borrelia Burgdorferi* – causing Lyme disease and *Bartonella*, causing Cat Scratch disease
- *Mycoplasma* – chronic respiratory and pelvic infections, joint pain, musculoskeletal problems

- *Streptococcus* – a history of chronic sore throats, tonsillitis, joint pain and other musculoskeletal problems
- *Rickettsia australis* — causing Queensland Tick Typhus
- Smouldering gum abscess from a range of bacteria.

Symptoms of bacterial infection:

- Fatigue unexplained by routine blood testing
- Multiple, ongoing symptoms that don't make sense
- Neurological symptoms; numbness, tingling and shooting pains
- Ongoing joint pains
- Persistent night sweats
- Swollen glands.

CFS patients with joint and musculoskeletal symptoms, may be suffering from the effects of *streptococcus or mycoplasma* infections. Underlying bacterial infection has been found to cause inflammatory syndromes, which include rheumatoid arthritis, fibromyalgia, scleroderma and others.

Lyme disease

Borrelia Burgdorferi, is the bacterial infection transferred by ticks that causes Lyme disease.

Diagnosing Lyme Disease is controversial in many countries. Sufferers of Lyme Disease can spend an average of seven years seeking a diagnosis. Lyme disease is known as 'The Great Imitator,' as it resembles many other diseases. Patients who are eventually diagnosed with Lyme disease often have gathered a long list of diagnoses ranging from psychosomatic, to rheumatoid arthritis, multiple sclerosis, Parkinson's disease and CFS, all unresponsive to treatment. This is caused in no small part by symptoms being peculiar, difficult to understand, changeable, coming and going over a long period of time. This exact scenario points towards the possibility of chronic bacterial infection. After a protracted period of suffering without any helpful treatment, testing for bacterial infection is a logical next step.

The Three Phases of Lyme disease

1. **Acute**: A bullseye type rash (*erythema migrans*) around a tick bite area can appear up to several weeks after the bite. By the time this symptom appears, the patient may have forgotten about the bite. The rash can last for a few weeks and then completely disappear.

2. **Chronic**: Vague flu-like symptoms, with fatigue and glandular swellings become persistent. Later, maybe many years later, the inflammatory stage begins.

Often this is joint pain, which is rarely connected with the tick bite years earlier. This can go on to develop fibromyalgia.

3. **Nervous**: The third stage of Lyme disease affects the nervous system, affecting cognition, with difficulty in concentration, memory loss and distorted or exaggerated sensory perception. More severe cases have intermittent paralysis, tics, vertigo and neuralgic pains. Cases of meningoencephalitis, cranial neuritis (Bell's palsy) and a range of undefinable neurological symptoms usually occur in undiagnosed, long-term cases.

Streptococcal Infection

Streptococcal infections are common in two scenarios:

4. A history, even many years before, of sore (strep) throats, or recurring severe tonsillitis with fever, which may have gone on to cause a chronic inflammatory state, especially in the joints, creating a pseudo-rheumatoid arthritis picture[3]. It can also cause other inflammatory musculoskeletal disorders like fibromyalgia and scleroderma.

5. Sometimes a patient describes having 'a dodgy tooth'

---

[3] *The Road Back: Rheumatoid Arthritis: Its Cause and its Treatment.* By Thomas McPherson-Brown, MD and Henry Scammell.

that never feels right, is sometimes sensitive to hot or cold food. There may also be recurring headaches on the same side as the tooth, which may have an old dental filling. These symptoms may mean a deep gum infection, yet dental X-rays can be inconclusive.

Mycoplasma

Infections caused by mycoplasma are also described by Dr Macpherson-Brown (See The Road Back Foundation in the Resources section at the end of this chapter), resulting in musculoskeletal inflammatory syndromes.

Rickettsia

Tick typhus, as it is commonly called, can be similar to Lyme Disease. Patients describe lethargy, dizziness and foggy thinking more often than the musculoskeletal or neurological symptoms.

IMPORTANT NOTE - Writing down in minute detail your health timeline may help you to recognise if you have had a previous bacterial infection. Have you ever had a tick bite? If you are a city dweller and you haven't been bushwalking, Lyme disease may not be your issue. Other things to look out for are events and *symptoms that preceded* your CFS symptoms, after an unusual skin rash, sore throat, tonsillitis, arthritis, travelling, or problems after dental work.

Treatment

There is no DIY (Do It Yourself) treatment for chronic bacterial infection, which must first be properly diagnosed, so that it can be treated with antibiotics. If you are in the situation of having had a variety of diagnoses and no successful treatment, it is reasonable for you to ask your doctor to test you for bacterial infection(s).

Medical authorities around the world have differing policies on the diagnosis and treatment of Lyme Disease, resulting in conflicting opinions from country to country. In Australia, health authorities do not acknowledge that Lyme disease exists, leaving thousands of patients without helpful treatment. A 'Lyme literate' doctor is able to order the appropriate test to check for Lyme Disease, and if positive, offer you antibiotic treatment.

Long-term antibiotics are often prescribed for Lyme Disease where there is evidence of *Borrelia* infection. A Lyme-literate doctor can prescribe these for you.

Complementary medicines for bacterial infection do have immune-stimulant action, but antibiotic therapy may be the treatment of choice.

Resources:

- *The International Lyme and Associated Diseases Society* (ILADS) www.ilads.org is a not-for-profit organisation of doctors, scientists and patients who are dedicated to informing and educating the international community about tick-borne diseases. The website offers informative videos and current information on Lyme and its related diseases.

- The TV documentary series *Under Our Skin* on Lyme Disease is informative and well worth viewing.

- *The Road Back Foundation.* The late Dr Thomas McPherson-Brown successfully treated over 10,000 patients with musculoskeletal disorders using long-term antibiotics. His work and patient network can be viewed at www.roadback.org

- Book: *The Road Back: Rheumatoid Arthritis: Its Cause and its Treatment.* By Thomas McPherson-Brown MD and Henry Scammell.

CHAPTER 5

BLOOD SUGAR DISORDERS

Blood sugar fluctuations, (different from diabetes) can be a factor with some CFS patients.

Low blood sugar (Hypoglycaemia), or unstable blood sugar, occurs in:

- Excessive sugar consumption and skipping meals
- Intestinal yeast overgrowth; see **Chapter 2: Gut Infections**
- Low reserves of the minerals chromium, manganese and zinc. Chromium is the most important as it is the main ingredient of the 'Glucose Tolerance Factor'.

Symptoms of glucose intolerance and hypoglycaemia are:

- Anxiety
- Dry mouth at night
- Foggy head
- Frequent night waking
- Hunger intolerance: not feeling right until eating
- Irritability
- Sugar cravings
- Trembling
- Unrefreshing sleep or sleep with unexplained patches of wakefulness.

A severe form of hypoglycaemia, a disorder called 'orthostatic intolerance' can trigger a sudden drop in blood sugar, which causes sudden fatigue, headache and nausea. Greg Page, of The Wiggles, had to retire from the stage due to this condition.

Tests

From your doctor:

- Blood chromium (GTF) levels
- Fasting blood sugar
- Glucose Tolerance Test.

From integrative doctors and other health professionals:

- Tissue Chromium levels via *Oligoscan*[4] or Hair Tissue Mineral Analysis.

Treatment

If followed well, dietary adjustment usually brings rapid improvement to symptoms. This is easily done without professional care. First though, check symptoms for yeast overgrowth, such as abdominal bloating, as described in **Chapter 2.**

Dietary measures:

- Avoid all sugar and refined carbohydrates (white bread, cakes and biscuits)
- Include protein (eggs, fish, meat, dairy) with each meal
- If you like fresh fruit, have it with protein
- Drink plenty of filtered water
- Eat a small meal or a snack of 100% whole grains and protein, every two hours. Ideal snacks are nuts, cheese and wholemeal crackers, fruit and yoghurt, vegetable sticks and hummus, a small fish tin, eggs, paté, baked beans

---

[4] See Appendix E

- If you wake during the night with hunger or blood sugar related symptoms, have a small snack as needed.

Supplements:

- Chromium, or any 'Glucose Tolerance Factor' supplement, available in retail outlets. Over time, this may help to reduce sugar cravings.

CHAPTER 6

COPPER OVERLOAD (COPPER TOXICITY)

Copper is a benign essential nutrient, which in tiny doses, we need for good health. You may ask what copper toxicity is doing in a book on chronic fatigue? For differing reasons, chronically high copper can occur in CFS sufferers. Excess copper causes a range of neurological, hormonal, mood, cognitive and gut symptoms. Copper accumulation can affect your liver, disturb your digestion and impede excretion via the gut and liver. This is why, once accumulated, copper can be difficult for the body to excrete.

High copper alone can keep you locked in a CFS pattern. If you have tried a range of treatments for CFS which haven't helped you, it may be unrecognised high copper affecting your liver function, which affects detoxification. Very high copper levels can affect zinc absorption which can in turn compound your health issues.

Symptoms of copper overload:

- Anxiety
- Autism Spectrum Disorders (ADHD, OCD, Asperger's Syndrome)
- Brain fog
- Depression
- Fatigue
- Fungal and yeast infections
- Headaches (hormonal)
- Hypersensitivity to chemicals and medications
- Hypothyroidism
- Insomnia and night terrors
- Irritable Bowel Syndrome (alternating constipation and diarrhoea)
- Migraines, especially hormonal
- Nausea
- Premenstrual syndrome (severe)
- Seizures
- Susceptibility to viral infections
- Tics and restless limbs.

Causes of Excess Copper

- Zinc deficiency
- Exposure to copper: environmental, copper based fungicides in swimming pools; copper water pipes; the contraceptive copper IUD
- A genetic condition called Kryptopyroluria (Pyrroles in urine) reduces the ability to properly absorb two essential nutrients for balancing copper levels; zinc and vitamin B6. Patients who test positive for Kryptopyroluria tend to be less responsive to treatment
- Artificial (xeno) oestrogens such as the oral contraceptive pill, plastics, chemicals, cosmetics, and industrial products. See the list below of xenoestrogen sources.

Copper and Liver Function

The liver is known as your body's 'chemical factory' and has many detoxifying functions by producing bile, which has three crucial functions:

1. Digest fats
2. Absorb nutrients in the gut
3. Bind with toxins and excrete them.

An excess of copper can impede these functions.

Blood tests may reveal elevated liver enzymes, which is a sign of liver inflammation, or if long-standing, a fatty liver. Even when liver enzymes are within normal range, bile output, normally produced by your liver and excreted via the gallbladder, may not be adequate. Bile colours your stool brown, so if you have pale stools, or you are constipated, your bile production is probably too low. If you suffer from sensitivity to chemicals, pharmaceutical drugs, or even natural medicines, this could be a sign that your liver is affected by elevated copper levels.

Copper and Oestrogen

Many women with CFS have high copper, coupled with excess oestrogen, called 'oestrogen dominance'. Oestrogen dominance is more common in women with high copper levels, because the liver's ability to clear oestrogen is partially blocked by the copper. Synthetic oestrogen (xenoestrogen) like the oral contraceptive pill (OCP) can cause copper accumulation. Other xenoestrogens, like plastics used in food preparation and storage, can also contribute to this problem.

Symptoms of oestrogen-related copper overload:

- Bloating
- Constipation
- Hormonally related breast pain and swelling

- Irritable Bowel Syndrome
- Rapid weight gain.

Tests

Tests that confirm copper overload are available from natural therapists and integrative doctors:

1. Hair Tissue Mineral Analysis - a sample of scalp hair is analysed. This will show how much copper your body is excreting. High copper levels will only show if there is enough available zinc.
2. *Oligoscan* [5] is a test which uses a Spectrophotometer (light meter) on the palm of the hand, to take a snapshot of the mineral levels in the body tissues a few millimetres under the skin. Copper levels show irrespective of the body's excretion ability.
3. Your doctor can order serum copper and zinc studies via a standard blood test.

---

[5] See Appendix C

Treatment

Normalising copper levels is relatively straightforward and usually helps to improve CFS symptoms.

First, look to avoid sources of copper you may be regularly exposed to:

- If your home has copper pipes and your drinking water tap hasn't been used for six or more hours, run cool water through the tap for at least 15 seconds before drinking.
- Install a water filter.
- High copper-containing foods are: dark chocolate, potatoes, shitake mushrooms, cashew nuts, sunflower seeds and tofu.
- Check your multivitamins for copper among its ingredients and select a non-copper containing supplement.

Xenoestrogen sources:

- Building supplies; wood preservatives, lubricants, adhesives and paints
- Food colourings and preservatives
- Fungicides
- Insecticides
- Oral Contraceptive Pill

- Plastics (Bisphenol A, Phthalates). Use glass or ceramic containers to store food, and when cooking or heating in microwave ovens.
- PVC
- Skincare products, including sunscreen (contains parabens).

Enhance liver function

In long-term CFS, improving liver function is a good starting point. Herbal bitters to help stimulate bile production:

- Bitter tasting vegetables — Endive, Amaranth greens, Broccoli Rabe and Dandelion Greens
- *Chelidonium* (Greater Celandine) herbal extract from health professionals
- Dandelion Coffee (dandelion root, not the leaf), to help with flushing the liver, particularly if you have IBS symptoms
- Lemon juice in warm water on waking
- Swedish Bitters.

Supplements

- Zinc and Vitamins C and B6 are natural antagonists to copper and need to be taken every day.

- Transdermal zinc cream improves zinc absorption through the skin rather than through the gut, which is especially helpful if you have high pyrroles (KPU). Apply once or twice daily for several months.

CHAPTER 7

MOULDS

Mould is commonplace in our lives. It grows in damp places like the bathroom, and cool dark areas, where black stains appear on walls. A bigger problem is water-damaged buildings which are the primary and hidden source of mould exposure.

Buildings become water-damaged after a flood, a burst water pipe, an accidental overflow, a leaking roof, leaky plumbing, all of which, unless thoroughly dried out, lead to invisible mould growth. The mould caused by water damage is not recognised until the building is examined in detail by trained professionals, as it grows in the cavities of buildings, such as the roof cavity, inside walls or the sub-floor space. Spores develop and grow for years, until the mould is discovered. This is one of the factors in what is commonly known as 'Sick Building Syndrome'.

Some people are more sensitive to mould than others. Genetic testing is available to diagnose mould *susceptibility*. When people who are genetically prone to mould sensitivity spend prolonged periods of time in buildings with visible mould, or a history of water damage, chronic health problems can develop.

Be in no doubt about the health risks of mould biotoxins. They affect the nervous system and cause severe symptoms. The problem here, is the length of time it takes to recognise and diagnose mould as a cause of CFS. If you have had a range of differing treatments over time without success, it is worth investigating if mould sensitivity and exposure could be a cause of your CFS.

Severe CFS from mould exposure can develop into a syndrome called *Chronic Inflammatory Response Syndrome* (CIRS), which is a serious form of CFS causing severe pain and debility.

Environment

It is not easy to recognise mould as being the reason for a health problem. Asking these questions may shed some light:

- Do your symptoms improve in dry weather?
- Do your symptoms worsen in wet weather?
- Do your symptoms improve or worsen when you leave home / arrive home?
- What happens to your symptoms when you go to work? Take a holiday?
- Does the building you live or work in have a history of water damage?
- Is there any particular place where your symptoms improve or worsen?

Food

Moulds in cheese and on the surface of cured meats that are safe, and can be washed off, but mould in all other foods is a health risk and should be discarded as soon as the slightest sign of mould is evident. Fresh and cooked foods should be refrigerated after 2 hours at room temperature, and leftovers should not be stored in the fridge for more than four days.

Symptoms

Neurological

Tremor; shooting pains; tingling; severe muscle cramps.

Cognitive

Brain fog; fatigue; headache.

Gastrointestinal

Nausea; metallic taste.

Cardiovascular

Nonsensical temperature sensitivity

Cold intolerance — even during hot weather

Night sweats.

Respiratory

Dry cough; sinusitis; skin rashes; sore throat; watery red eyes; wheezing.

Tests

The *Mould Biotoxin Panel* is a urine test your health professional can order for you.

Genetic test for halotypes: '11-3-52B" or "4-3-53'

Treatment

- If your CFS is caused by, or affected by, biotoxins from mould, *removing yourself from the source of the problem is essential in order for you to recover.*

- If there are visible black stains in any building you spend time in, treat the stains by scrubbing the mould off and applying vinegar, which kills mould spores. Bleach is harmful to inhale and does bleach the stain but does not kill mould spores. CFS sufferers should not remove this mould themselves.

- If a water damaged building isn't fully dried out, repaired and the mould properly remediated by professionals, mould sensitive CFS sufferers using that building will not be able to recover.

- Buildings with suspected water damage need specialist inspectors to recognise and assess your building for mould and provide a report so that remedial action can be taken. Mould found in building cavities must be treated by a qualified mould-removal technician. Even if you don't have CFS, make sure you are out of the building while cleaning takes place, as mould spores can be liberated during their removal and affect your health.

- Having identified and addressed environmental moulds, complete recovery can only occur once the mould biotoxins *in your body* have been excreted. Your doctor may be able to prescribe medication to alleviate symptoms, such as nystatin. Some doctors prescribe a medication called *Cholestyramine*, an old cholesterol-lowering drug, which acts as a mould biotoxin binder in the gut, and assists in excretion of those toxins.

- A binding or chelating agent after meals like Bentonite clay, diatomaceous earth, or *Xeolite* taken three times daily can help to excrete moulds.
- Professional care is needed to treat mould biotoxins. See a practitioner who has experience in treating mould toxicity, or CIRS.

Resources:

- Dr Ritchie Shoemaker is a pioneer of mould biotoxin treatment and has written many books on the subject. See 'Surviving Mold' www.survivingmold.com
- Book: *Healthy Home Healthy Family - Is where you life affecting your health?* By Nicole Bijlsma

CHAPTER 8

FIBROMYALGIA

Fibromyalgia is a commonly misunderstood, sometimes misdiagnosed rheumatic disease. It is nine times more common among women than men, usually occuring between the ages of 40 and 60. It is more common in Caucasians than other races, and is one of the most common disorders treated by rheumatologists. Fibromyalgia is not life-threatening, nor does it cause physical deformities. Laboratory tests are usually within normal range. In fact, most people with fibromyalgia look well and fit, making it difficult to account for the degree of clinical suffering they are experiencing, yet 10 - 30 per cent of fibromyalgia patients are disabled to some degree, because of the severity of their symptoms.

Fibromyalgia is not limited to a single cause. A majority of patients identify a flu-like or viral illness and often respond well to antiviral treatment. Some patients' fibromyalgia has been triggered by physical trauma/injury. In others, emotional stress is a precursor to the onset of symptoms.

Symptoms

- Aching and pain felt in the muscles (not joints)
- Depression
- Fatigue
- Headaches
- Irritable bowel syndrome
- Raynaud's phenomenon (cold, numb pale extremities, commonly seen as a 'glove and stocking effect)
- Sleep disorders
- Stiffness.

Trigger Points

The sites of pain located in specific areas are called trigger points, where the ligament attaches muscle to the bone. There are 18 tender point locations in the body. Sensitivity at 11 of these points defines a diagnosis of fibromyalgia.

Infection?

The connection between fibromyalgia and infection has been well studied, especially in relation to Lyme disease, mycoplasma, *Chlamydia pneumoniae,* Hepatitis C, Parvovirus B19, HIV, and the Epstein-Barr virus. This suggests that fibromyalgia is not an entity in itself, but a symptom of an underlying, difficult to identify, infection. I often see an association with Epstein-Barr virus and fibromyalgia in patients.

Some infections, in particular unresolved viral infections, the spirochete (*Borrelia*) infection of Lyme Disease, and mycoplasma infections, require highly specialised laboratory tests. Your own timeline of health events can be quite informative before having such tests. See **Chapter 4: Bacterial Infection.**

Toxicity

Patients who have high levels of tissue Cadmium and Lead can have fibromyalgia symptoms.

Treatment

There is no end to the number of products available to help with fibromyalgia symptoms. While it is best to seek professional care, these easily available products may help:

Magnesium

Transdermal Magnesium Sulphate (either cream or oil), gives some relief for most sufferers of fibromyalgia. When applied to the skin, magnesium absorbs more easily into the muscle fibres and appears to be more effective than oral magnesium supplements.

Herbal Anti-inflammatories

Herbal medicines can help to relieve the pain of fibromyalgia. Many are available over the counter, or a health professional can make up an individualised formula for you.

Common herbal anti-inflammatories:

- Turmeric (containing curcumin)
- White willow bark
- Boswelia
- Ginger.

Herbal Relaxants (available in tablet or liquid form).

To relax the body and improve sleep quality:

- Californian poppy
- Passionflower
- Skullcap
- Valerian.

Amino acids

L-tryptophan, 5 HTP (5 hydroxy-tryptophan) can calm hypersensitive nerve fibres and reduce pain.

A recent supplement showing some positive results for pain is PEA (Palmitoylethanolamide). This also has a small role in helping depression as well as nerve pain in particular, after several weeks of supplementation.

Resources:

- *The Road Back Foundation.* The late Dr Thomas McPherson-Brown successfully treated over 10,000 patients with musculoskeletal disorders using long-term antibiotics. His work and patient network can be viewed at www.roadback.org
- Book: *The Road Back: Rheumatoid Arthritis: Its Cause and its Treatment,* by Thomas McPherson-Brown, MD and Henry Scammell.
- *The International Lyme and Associated Diseases Society* (ILADS) www.ilads.org is a not-for-profit organisation of doctors, scientists and patients who are dedicated to informing and educating the international community about tick-borne diseases. The website offers informative videos and current information on Lyme and its related diseases.
- The TV documentary series *Under Our Skin* on Lyme Disease is informative and well worth viewing.

CHAPTER 9

HEAVY METAL TOXICITY

Heavy metal toxicity means that small amounts of toxic elements have accumulated in body tissues and caused symptoms that compromise your health. For example, elevated lead levels affect mental function in children. Another common heavy metal that causes health issues is mercury, which can accumulate in people who have amalgam (silver) fillings in their teeth, which slowly leaches out over time.

We are all unavoidably exposed to heavy metals. Ideally, our bodies excrete toxic substances like heavy metals and we get through life in good health. The problem with heavy metals is that they are neurotoxic, carcinogenic and can trigger autoimmune disease. Some people tolerate heavy metal loads better than others. In susceptible people, toxic substances are not well excreted and accumulate in body tissues. An excess of one or more heavy metals can contribute to symptoms of CFS, especially if liver detoxification or gut elimination is compromised.

While heavy metals are a perennial problem in human health, one cannot assume heavy metals are the cause of all chronic health problems. It is important to assess heavy metal status in chronic disease to discern if they are the cause of a person's specific health issues.

Health professionals are trained to assess if heavy metals are an underlying cause of disease. It is not recommended that patients have tests done and analyse the results themselves. If only it were that simple!

The impact of heavy metals on human health is a huge topic and cannot be covered fully here.

See Chapter 6: Copper Overload.

Symptoms

While the symptoms listed below are common to chronic fatigue, it is not safe to assume your CFS symptoms are caused by heavy metals unless testing has confirmed elevated levels.

Potential Symptom	Toxic Element
Fatigue	Aluminium, lead, mercury, cadmium
Muscle pain	Aluminium, lead, cadmium
Unrefreshing sleep	Cadmium
Oversensitivity to temperature, medications, household cleaners, perfumes, herbs	Mercury
Leaky gut syndrome (see Ch 2)	Mercury
Brain fog	Mercury, lead, aluminium, copper

Tests

'Heavy metals' have become a buzzword to the point that some patients attend clinic asking for a "heavy metal detox". Before entering into heavy metal detoxification programs, it is important to establish if heavy metals are affecting you. Until testing reveals specific heavy metal levels and are properly assessed by a qualified health professional, one cannot assume heavy metals are the cause of a person's symptoms.

Available tests:

Oligoscan and Hair Tissue Mineral Analysis are used to assess chronic long term accumulation of toxic elements. Urine and blood tests measure acute, short-term exposures.

- *Oligoscan* [6], (So/Check in Europe) uses spectrophotometry; a simple procedure which measures mineral and toxic element levels that have accumulated over time.
- Hair Tissue Mineral Analysis: measures the levels of excretion of a small sample of uncoloured scalp hair .
- Blood and urine tests measure heavy metal levels when there has been a recent, acute exposure.

Hair, urine and blood, measure the excretion capacity of an individual. CFS patients tend not excrete toxins well, which means excretory pathology tests may understate the true toxic load.

Treatment

Treatment consists of three phases:

1. Avoid sources
2. Improve nutrition
3. Enhance detoxification pathways

---

[6] See Appendices B & C

Avoid Sources

It can take some detective work to identify heavy metal sources you are in contact with, including air pollution. Lifestyle factors can influence an individual's ability to excrete unwanted heavy metals. Poor diet, low quality drinking water and air pollution are a few factors which influence heavy metal accumulation. With awareness, individuals can begin to identify possible exposure to some heavy metals, and adjust their lifestyle.

Sources of Common Heavy Metal Exposures

Aluminium:	Deodorant, cosmetics, drinking water, antacids.
Antimony:	Flame retardants in most home furnishings, PET water bottles, food grade plastic containers.
Arsenic:	Chicken feed, insecticides, fungicides, seafood, wood preservatives (treated pine), ground water, ceramics, glass, tobacco, pigments, textiles, paper, metal adhesives.
Cadmium:	Petrol exhaust fumes, cigarette smoke, welding rods, soil, therefore in some foods.

Aluminium:	Deodorant, cosmetics, drinking water, antacids.
Copper:	Copper water pipes, brass taps, town water supplies, swimming pool fungicides, wood, leather and fabric preservatives.
Lead:	Fossil fuels, leaded paint, leaded petrol, solder, pipes, glazes, pigments, ceramics, cosmetics, LED lights, batteries, ammunition.
Mercury:	Silver amalgam tooth fillings, seafood, effluent from coal-fired power stations, damaged fluorescent lights, skin lightening creams, antibacterial agents, thimerosal, paints, pigments, tattoo dyes, some anti-fungal agents.

For more information see: Agency For Toxic Substances and Disease Registry https://www.atsdr.cdc.gov

Improve Nutrition

Chronic Heavy metal accumulation can occur in your body because you may have too few protective nutrients. Low levels of zinc, selenium, iodine and silica can all predispose to heavy metal accumulation. Supplementing with these minerals can help offset the effects of heavy metal body loads.

Nutrient minerals that oppose toxic minerals:

Toxic heavy metal	Nutrient mineral
Aluminium	Silica
Antimony	Chromium
Cadmium	Zinc, Selenium
Copper	Zinc, Molybdenum
Lead	Calcium
Mercury	Selenium, Iodine

3. Detoxification Pathways

Liver

Liver detoxification is essential to assist your body's elimination processes. Your liver is your body's filtration system, so the filter needs to be regularly cleansed, enabling toxic materials to be transported out of the liver aided by bile, and into the intestine for excretion. Herbal bitters are an excellent way to facilitate this.

Herbal bitters that stimulate bile production and improve gut function

- Bitter tasting vegetables — Endive, Amaranth greens, Broccoli Rabe and Dandelion Greens

- *Chelidonium* (Greater Celandine) is a herbal extract available from health professionals
- Dandelion Coffee (dandelion root, not the leaf), helps to flush high copper levels through the liver
- Lemon juice in warm water on waking
- Swedish Bitters.

Kidneys

Drink plenty of non-fluoridated and non-chlorinated water. The best water has mineral salts: sodium, magnesium, potassium, which keep the water slightly alkaline. A good quality water filter will help to achieve this.

Skin

Your largest elimination organ is your skin, through perspiration. If you don't sweat much, then one of your most important detoxification outlets needs to be stimulated. Sweating can be achieved through vigorous exercise, infrared saunas, sweat lodges, or other methods that raise body temperature. Saunas are available in health spas and some gyms, or you can buy a home sauna — a worthwhile investment for anyone with chronic health issues, and it can be used by the whole family.

Naturally occurring substances that can also help detoxification of heavy metals:

- Chlorella
- Coriander
- Diatomaceous Earth, Bentonite Clay, Xeolites
- Liposomal Glutathione.

Hyperthermia therapy, also called thermal medicine or thermotherapy, is available at specialised treatment centres to treat rheumatological, chronic inflammatory disorders and some cancers. Body tissue is exposed to high temperature, aimed at stimulating the body's immune system to stimulate healing. It can be used in conjunction with conventional treatments and is available through a referral from your healthcare professional.

Resources

- The not-for-profit *Environmental Working Group:* https://www.ewg.org produces scientific papers on environmental contamination sources, plus consumer reports on the safest products to use.
- Book: Rapp, Dr D., *Our Toxic World, A Wake Up Call*, Environmental Medical Research Foundation, NY, 2004

CHAPTER 10

CHEMICALS AND SENSITIVITY

Chemical exposure has a long history in relation to our health, and the effects can be far-reaching. If our grandparents were exposed to DDT, it can still affect our health now. Chemicals are a health problem, as they are capable of reaching into the energy production centre of our cells, (mitochondria), which can directly affect cell function and therefore energy levels.

Currently, upwards of 80,000 chemicals are used in industry, resulting in environmental contamination and creating the potential to adversely affect health. Of great concern, is that fewer than one per cent of these chemicals have been tested and/or regulated.[7]

Many chemicals do not degrade and can be found in soil decades after their use. These are called 'Persistent Organic Pollutants' or POPs. The most widely spread chemical internationally is the everyday weedkiller 'broad spectrum herbicide' glyphosate. The safety of glyphosate is controversial, but many studies have confirmed serious health risks related to glyphosate in the food chain. With the use of specialised pathology tests, chemicals like glyphosate can be detected in the human body. While many of the POP's (see table below) are now banned, even if they were used decades ago, they may still be present in significant amounts in the environment.

Chemical Exposure

Environmentally, air pollution is a growing problem, but most chemicals that we are exposed to, are in our own homes! Until recently, chemical residues in CFS patients have been impossible to detect until symptoms develop.

---

[7] https://www.sciencedaily.com/releases/2016/04/160426101616.htm

Fortunately, affordable tests are now available to identify some common chemical exposures. **See Tests below.**

Toxic chemicals are found in:

* Cleaning products
* Cosmetics
* Garden products
* Personal care products.

Chemicals in Household Products

Product	Ingredient
Ant Killer	Dieldrin
Cockroach Bomb	Chlordane; Heptachlor
Flea Shampoo	Dieldrin, Lindane
Fly Spray	Lindane or DDT
Insect Repellant	Hexachlorophene
Seed Dressing	Lindane
Snail and Slug Killer	Lindane
Termite Spray	Chlordane, Heptachlor, Dieldrin
Vegetable & Flower Dusts	DDT, Lindane
Wood preservative	Pentachlorophenol
Weed killer	Glyphosate ('Round Up')

Sensitivity

When considering the increasing prevalence of people with CFS, the theme of 'sensitivity' arises. Sufferers of CFS become oversensitive to a particular element: commonly, it is a virus. **See Chapter 1: Post-Viral Syndromes.**

It can also be a toxin that is man-made or naturally occurring. Toxic overload occurs when the normal detoxification pathways stop working efficiently. These pathways are the kidneys, liver, gut and the skin. As these pathways become congested, chemical sensitivity develops.

Oversensitivity develops in:

- Intestines
- Immune system
- Detoxification (methylation) pathways
- Nervous system.

If a chemical or chemicals can be identified, then the treatment pathway is clearer.

Symptoms

Extreme chemical sensitivity can lead to a profoundly limited and isolated lifestyle, as this situation compels people to live extremely simplified lives away from all possible sources of pollution in order to avoid aggravation of their symptoms.

These symptoms typify what many CFS sufferers experience:

- Asthma
- Confusion
- Fatigue
- Headaches
- Hypersensitivity to specific chemicals eg perfumes
- Memory loss
- Muscle pain
- Rashes.

Tests

CFS sufferers who have been unresponsive to treatment thus far, may benefit from testing to identify specific chemicals, which has recently become more affordable and available from health professionals.

The *Organic Acid Test* (OAT) is a simple urine test which measures the by-products of metabolism and detects the genetic markers which make individuals more susceptible to the effect of chemicals.

Treatment

Treatment for chemical sensitivity is quite similar to treatment for heavy metal toxicity, based on three stages:

1. *Avoid the source of exposure wherever possible*

This is one area of treatment where you can exert a large amount of control on the potentially harmful chemicals to which you are exposed. A huge reduction of your chemical load can be accomplished by exchanging traditional home cleaning and personal care products for non-toxic, organic products. This will benefit your whole family as well.

2. *Eat Clean Food*

Grow your own food where possible. Container gardening is an option; start small, with a pot of parsley on the windowsill! In the garden, throw your chemicals out and introduce permaculture-type gardening methods to find alternative solutions to weed control. If you don't have a garden, buy organic food where possible and support local farmer's markets, where you can check gardening methods with the growers at the point of purchase. Supporting organic producers sends a strong message to retailers, who are increasingly supplying organic products at affordable prices.

Watchdog: You can check the safety of food brands, personal care and many other products from the not-for-profit organisation Environmental Working Group ewg.org. When we checked the site at the time of writing there was a report on the detection of glyphosate in store-bought hummus.

3. *Provide sufficient nutrients*

Nutrients in adequate levels help the body eliminate substances that are compromising health. Zinc, magnesium, selenium, vitamin C and B group vitamins are all crucial.

See also Detoxification via liver, skin and kidneys, in the last paragraphs of **Chapter 9.** Many patients with chemical sensitivity have gut dysbiosis and require targeted antimicrobials and probiotics. **See Chapter 2: Gut Infections.**

Resources

- Book: *Healthy Home Healthy Family; Is Where You are Living Affecting Your Health?* by Nicole Bijlsma

- Environmental Working Group ewg.org

CHAPTER 11

BOTOX AND OTHER MEDICATIONS

If you, or someone you know, is thinking of having cosmetic *Botox* injections, it is worth knowing that *Botox* is derived from the bacteria *Clostridium botulinum,* the organism that causes a life-threatening illness called Botulism, or 'Impaired Neuronal Communication Syndrome'. This rare disease is contracted via contact with the bacteria in food that is bottled or canned, and through broken skin. Symptoms begin with weakness, blurry vision, fatigue, and difficulty speaking.

Some of my clients who have had *Botox* beauty treatments have learned the hard way, presenting with these symptoms:

- Blurry or double vision
- Difficulty breathing
- Difficulty swallowing
- Dry mouth
- Eyelid droop
- Fatigue
- Muscle weakness and paralysis
- Muscle twitching
- Slow reflexes
- Slurred speech
- Vertigo
- Weakness.

Treatment

There are much safer and more effective ways to enhance beauty than receiving *Botox* injections. Women concerned about their appearance can greatly benefit from simple health measures like three healthy meals per day, daily fruit and vegetable juicing, plenty of filtered water, regular exercise and at least eight hours of good quality sleep every night.

When there is a clear 'before and after' reaction that can easily identify a toxin like *Botox*, an individual detoxification medicine is very effective. An individualised protocol to detoxify the effects of Botox is available from some health professionals.

Potentially, any prescribed medication can activate a set of symptoms, which can signal the start of ongoing health issues.

Commonly, these are:

- *Lyrica* (pregabalin), originally used as an anticonvulsant for epilepsy by slowing down impulses in the brain that cause seizures
- Antidepressants – SSRIs
- Oral Contraceptive Pill: **see Chapter 7: Copper Toxicity.**

With the help of writing down your health timeline, you may recognise 'before symptoms and after symptoms', which may turn out to be a key to your recovery.

CHAPTER 12

TRAUMA

Although I have emphasised that the emotional component of CFS is far more likely to be the *result* of having CFS rather than the cause of it, the impact of long-term stress must still be considered. Ongoing stress can lead to a person staying in a state of high alert, even after the event itself has passed. Over time, this has an exhausting effect and is recognised as adrenal exhaustion.

Thankfully, unresolved trauma is recognised nowadays as Post-Traumatic Stress Disorder (PTSD). This may well be a part of the picture of the CFS sufferer. A history of abuse, emotional shock, profound life situations, military service, a prolonged period of conflict, at work, home, or in the neighbourhood may contribute to CFS.

The nervous system can carry the memory of shock from any time in life going many years back, even to childhood. You may have heard of the 'body/mind connection'. Even though your conscious mind has 'moved on,' the trauma can still be affecting you. As CFS is usually more than a single problem, trauma or shock may be a significant factor. Left unrecognised and treated, it could be an impediment to recovery.

Treatment

Unresolved and seemingly unmanageable emotional issues are best dealt with in the hands of health professionals. Where professional help is not possible or desirable, some simple techniques that you can safely implement at home, may be helpful.

Therapeutic Journaling

The power and helpfulness of writing down your feelings takes just a pencil and paper and a little time. 'Therapeutic journaling', brought to light by American psychologist James Pennebaker, is based on the idea that how a person processes the negative events in their life, affects how well they emerge from those events. Externalising thoughts and feelings can be surprisingly therapeutic. This pdf outlining the process can be downloaded free: http://projects.hsl.wisc.edu/SERVICE/modules/12/M12_CT_TherapeuticJournaling.pdf

Cybertherapy

Online counselling is a proven helpful method, particularly for people who cannot see a professional in person, due to finances, distance, shyness, disability, lack of time or other issues. *MoodGym* moodgym.com.au is a 24–hour online self-help interactive programme designed to help users manage symptoms of depression and anxiety. It is a scientifically based programme developed by researchers at the Australian National University (ANU). This programme has become quite successful, equalling the benefits of face-to-face sessions. *MoodGym* now has over one million users worldwide.

EFT/Tapping

This method of mental health care is a new area of therapy based on the Chinese Medicine meridians[8], or energy pathways in the body. EFT (Emotional Freedom

---

[8] Meridians are a subtle anatomy well known in Traditional Chinese Medicine

Technique) is becoming more accepted in the world of psychology and a substantial body of research is being gathered in order to gain more acceptance in mainstream medicine. Doctor Peta Stapleton from Bond University, Queensland Australia https://petastapleton.com is spearheading international research. Her website has many resources if you are interested in exploring this fascinating area of mental health.

You can watch her Ted Talk at TEDx Robina on the Gold Coast in Queensland: Is *Therapy Facing a Revolution?* at www.youtube.com/watch?v=0Vu0Tibt1bQ

CHAPTER 13

WHAT ELSE?

I realise how truly disheartening it can be when you are not seeing improvement after yet another strategy you have tried has failed. **This does not mean that you cannot be helped.** Be assured that there are uncommon types of CFS not mentioned here, and *combinations of causes* that may take time and precision to recognise. Whether you have suffered from CFS for one or 20 years, your chances of recovery are the same — *if the cause or causes can be clearly identified.*

If none of what you have read here seems to fit your symptoms, I encourage you to rethink your history in more detail, because there is likely to be something in your timeline that you haven't yet recalled. Ask your partner, a parent, any family member or a person you spent time with who might remember what happened with your health that you don't. What do they remember about when you first became unwell? This information could be vital to understanding the cause of your CFS and point towards further testing to help develop an individualised treatment programme for you.

No single treatment can benefit every CFS sufferer. A common mistake for CFS (and other syndromes), is to look for a single cause or treatment. For CFS treatment to be successful, it needs to be individualised, addressing your own unique set of symptoms and not a 'one size fits all' treatment.

Provided you have had full medical testing and assessment, eliminating the possibility of other disease, seeing a practitioner who is familiar with treating CFS and uses the wide range of therapies needed for each case, is a natural next step.

I wish you the best possible recovery from your CFS.

APPENDICES

APPENDIX A
HOMEMADE PROBIOTICS

Probiotic foods can be cheaply and easily made at home, and are arguably equally or more effective as costly commercial probiotics. This is a significant factor for people who have been unwell for a prolonged period of time, as affordability of treatments can become a real challenge.

This is one area when sufferers can do a lot to help their recovery — help to restore healthy gut bacteria.

There are many probiotic foods:

- **Kefir yoghurt**
- **Pickles**
- **Sauerkraut**

Other probiotics can be made as drinks, such as Kombucha, but here the focus is on probiotic foods.

If you tolerate dairy, you can make your own yoghurt using *kefir*. Kefir yoghurt is a 'super food' which is superior to commercial probiotics and yoghurts. It can be made at home for the cost of the milk used in making it, instead of paying up to $50 for probiotics. You can buy kefir grains online, or at your local health food store.

If you are sensitive to dairy products, you can use goats milk, coconut milk or rice milk (not long-life) to make delicious kefir yoghurt. As with probiotic supplements, start taking just a couple of teaspoons of kefir at first, and increase after a few days as tolerated. Too much too soon can aggravate your symptoms, because the probiotic organisms compete with the candida yeast for territory: you don't want to start a battle in your gut.

Organisms Found In Kefir Yoghurt

The range of organisms found in Kefir yoghurt is wider than any probiotic you can purchase. It contains more than thirty types of lactobacilli, acetobacter, streptococci, lactobacilli and yeasts.

Once you have your own **Kefir grain**, you can make your own yoghurt with fresh milk at room temperature, because it **regenerates perpetually in fresh milk, at room temperature.** Kefir grains do not deteriorate; all that is required is fresh milk of your choice and five minutes of your time each day.

Kefir can be made at any temperature from 4 to 40°C. At lower temperatures it takes longer to set. As soon as you get your grain, put it in half a cup of cow, goat, soy or coconut milk, cover, and leave on the kitchen bench until it thickens.

Kefir yoghurt is runnier than commercial yoghurt. As the grain grows, it will set larger quantities of milk. Eventually the grain will grow so that it sets up to one litre of your preferred milk at a time. The first few batches of Kefir you make may not yield as much yoghurt, or taste as good as later, as the grains will be "waking up".

How To Make Kefir Yoghurt

Utensils:

- A 500 ml ceramic or glass container with a cover
- A container to store kefir in the fridge
- A sieve to strain the freshly made Kefir

Use ANY type of milk (including coconut, soy, rice milk, powdered, sheep and goats') **except long life milks.**

Method:

1. Put the Kefir grains in your container, add your preferred milk and cover
2. Add a dessert spoon of milk powder if you prefer

thicker yoghurt.

3. Stir every 12 hours or so. Setting time will vary, from one to several days, according to the strength of the grain, room temperature and the type of milk.

4. When set, pour through a sieve, and retain the kefir grain.

5. Spoon unwashed grains back into the 500 ml jar and repeat the process. Wash utensils in **unchlorinated** water.

NB. Never heat the milk, as excess temperature is one of the few things that will kill the grains. Similarly, never use bleaches or detergents for cleaning the utensils you use when making Kefir, as these may kill or taint the grain.

Sharing grains:

When the grains are about the size of a walnut, small pieces drop off readily. A grain the size of 1 mm diameter is enough to grow new grains! Take a small grain and grow it for a week in the same jar, then pass it on when it's bigger.

Storing Grains:

Store in the refrigerator in a jar covered with filtered, unchlorinated water. Refresh the water every week. **USE CLEAN WATER:** CHLORINATED TOWN WATER MAY DAMAGE THE GRAINS.

Not Sure How to Start?

To see a simple demonstration: http://www.youtube.com/watch?v=g8inJzX-6yE

References:

- *Encyclopaedia of Food Science & Food Technology & Nutrition* 5 ISBN: 0-12-226855-5, ACADEMIC PRESS -> Food Technology and Nutrition: "Kefir" pp 1804-1808.
- *International Journal of Systematic Bacteriology* 44 (3) 435-439 (1994) [21 ref. En] — * two new organisms recently discovered!

Other Probiotic Foods:

Sauerkraut, or pickled cabbage, aids digestion and develops good gut bacteria. Eat a few tablespoons or more with lunch and dinner. If you don't like the taste, mix it with your mashed potatoes, **but don't let it heat up**, as heat will kill the beneficial bacteria. Eating this simple food daily could go a long way to improving your gut function.

You do need to make sauerkraut yourself though, because commercially available sauerkraut may have been pasteurised, which kills the very bacteria that you need. There are many types of sauerkraut. The Internet is laden with recipes on how to make it. Basically, it involves pounding the head of a cabbage mixed with some salt and letting it ferment.

Kimchi (Korean Sauerkraut) - Makes one quart (1200mls)

1 head Wombok cabbage (also known as Napa, or Chinese cabbage)
1 bunch spring onions, chopped
1 cup grated carrot
½ cup grated daikon radish (optional)
1 tablespoon of freshly grated ginger
3 cloves of garlic, peeled and minced
½ teaspoon of dried chilli flakes
1 teaspoon of salt
4 tablespoons of whey, or one additional teaspoon of salt

Japanese Sauerkraut

1 head Wombok (Napa, or Chinese Cabbage) cored and finely shredded
1 bunch green onions, chopped
2 tablespoons of soya sauce
2 tablespoons of freshly squeezed lemon juice
1 teaspoon of sea salt
2 tablespoons of whey (from making kefir)
If whey is not available, use another teaspoon of salt

Method for both recipes

Put all the ingredients in a bowl and pound with a wooden pounder, meat hammer, or the pestle from a mortar and pestle until there is lots of juice. Place in a one litre wide mouthed glass or ceramic container, and press down firmly until the juice rises above the cabbage, by about one centimetre. There should be a couple of centimetres of space below the top of the container. Cover and leave at room temperature for three days, then store in the fridge.

Salsa Vegetable Pickle (no cooking required)

1 kg tomatoes, 1 capsicum, 1 red onion, 4 cloves of garlic, fresh coriander
1-2 teaspoons chillies (optional)
Wash and chop everything up, mix it all together, pack tightly into a jar, leaving a 1 cm space at the top. Cover, but don't seal. In a few days bubbles will start to appear. The jar may overflow, so place it on a plate. When the bubbling settles, seal the jar and it's ready to eat.

To stop further fermentation store in the fridge. Start eating small quantities and gradually increase the amount. Eat within two weeks.

APPENDIX B
TESTS

There is no standard test to confirm a diagnosis of CFS. The tests below are the specialised tests of preference used to investigate CFS. These are not standard blood pathology tests. Always see your doctor for a full medical assessment before considering specialised pathology tests.

Test Name	Test Type	Components tested
Oligoscan	Spectrophotometry (light metre placed on the palm)	Toxic elements, minerals, vitamins
Hair Tissue Mineral Analysis	Scalp hair	Toxic elements, minerals
Organic Acids	Urine test	Metabolic panel for factors detoxification, infection, toxins
Moulds, Mycotoxins, biotoxins	Urine test	Mould residues

Test Name	Test Type	Components tested
Complete Gut Microbiome	Stool test	Gut infections, bacteria and other markers
Chemical Panel	Urine test	Synthetic chemicals
IgG food sensitivity panel	Blood/Skin prick	Food sensitivity reactions
Tick borne diseases panel or Western Blot panel	Blood test	Tick borne antigens

APPENDIX C
OLIGOSCAN
(SPECTROPHOTOMETRY)

An *Oligoscan* is a test conducted in-consultation by placing a handheld device called a spectrophotometer against the skin of the palm, to measure minerals, vitamins and toxic element levels in body tissue. The technology uses the infrared light spectrum, through spectrophotometry, which passes through the skin to reflect the mineral and vitamin content there.

Where standard blood tests measure current blood levels of constituents, *tissue* levels reveal how the body is able to absorb and retain substances from the blood into the tissues, by measuring the constituents of the intracellular spaces.

It is a testing procedure only, is painless and takes less than 10 seconds. Results are correlated with a patient's presenting symptoms by a trained professional.

In most countries the device is known as an '*Oligoscan*', but in Europe is called 'So/Check'.

RESOURCES

Infections

The International Lyme and Associated Diseases Society (ILADS) www.ilads.org is a not-for-profit organisation of doctors, scientists and patients who are dedicated to informing and educating the international community about tick-borne diseases. The website offers informative videos and current information on Lyme and its related diseases.

TV documentary series 'Under Our Skin' on Lyme Disease

The Road Back Foundation. The late Dr Thomas McPherson-Brown successfully treated over 10,000 patients with musculoskeletal disorders using long-term antibiotics. His work and patient network can be viewed at www.roadback.org.

Book: *The Road Back: Rheumatoid Arthritis: Its Cause and its Treatment.* By Thomas McPherson-Brown, MD Henry Scammell.

Surviving Mold www.survivingmold.com Dr Ritchie Shoemaker, a US doctor is a pioneer of mould biotoxin treatment and has written many books on the subject.

Environment

Book: *Healthy Home Healthy Family - Is where you live affecting your health?* By Nicole Bijlsma ISBN-10: 0648194795 Australian College Enviro Sci (February 5, 2018)

Agency For Toxic Substances and Disease Registry
https://www.atsdr.cdc.gov

Environmental Working Group: https://www.ewg.org is a not-for-profit organisation that produces scientific papers on environmental contamination sources, plus consumer reports on the safest products to use.

Book: Rapp, Dr D, *Our Toxic World, A Wake Up Call,* Environmental Medical Research Foundation. ISBN-13 : 978-1880509081 NY, 2004

Books: Lourie B. and Smith R., *Slow Death By Rubber Duck* Knopf Canada; Expanded, Updated Edition (January 15, 2019) ISBN-13 : 978-0735275706

ToxInToxOut, St Marys, NY, 2013, ISBN978-1-250-05133-2

Emotional Support

MoodGym moodgym.com.au An interactive self-help site which helps you to learn and practise skills which can help to prevent and manage symptoms of depression and anxiety.

Therapeutic Journaling: James W. Pennebaker
https://pennebaker.socialpsychology.org

EFT (Emotional Freedom Technique) Doctor Peta Stapleton Bond University, Queensland Australia https://petastapleton.com conducts an international research programme.

Centers of Disease Control and Prevention

What is ME/CFS?

www.cdc.gov/me-cfs/about/

Symptoms of ME/CFS

www.cdc.gov/me-cfs/symptoms-diagnosis/symptoms.html

Symptoms and Diagnosis of ME/CFS

www.cdc.gov/me-cfs/symptoms-diagnosis/

Diagnosis of ME/CFS

www.cdc.gov/me-cfs/symptoms-diagnosis.diagnosis.html

Treatment of ME/CFS

www.cdc.gov/me-cfs/treatment/

Possible Causes Myalgic Encephalomyelitis/Chronic Fatigue Syndrome

www.cdc.gov/me-cfs/about/possible-causes.html

Living With ME/CFS

www.cdc.gov/me-cfs/patient-stories/

Video content highlighting the unique issues faced by people with ME/CFS, and their stories in their own voices.

FURTHER READING

Brownstein, D, Overcoming Thyroid Disorders, 3rd ed, *Medical Alternative Press,* MI USA, 2014 ISBN 978-0-9660882-2-9

Gamble, J, *The Treatment of Irritable Bowel Syndrome, Mastering Homeopathy 2:* Karuna Publishing, 2006 ISBN0-9752473-1-0

Obstacles to Cure: Toxicity, Deficiency and Infection, Karuna Publishing, 2010, ISBN 9780975247334

Kharrazian, D, *Why Do I still Have Thyroid Symptoms When my Lab Tests are Normal?* Elephant Press, CA, 2010 ISBN978-0-9856904-0-3

MacPherson-Brown, T., Scammell, H., Book: *The Road Back: Rheumatoid Arthritis: Its Cause and its Treatment.* ISBN-10 : 0871315432 M Evans & Co; First Printing Edition (August 8, 1988)

Pfeiffer, C., *Mental and Elemental Nutrients: A Physician's Guide to Nutrition and Health Care* ISBN 10 0879831146 Keats Pub, New Canaan, Ct 1976

Rapp, Dr D, O*ur Toxic World, A Wake Up Call,*
Environmental Medical Research Foundation. ISBN-13
: 978-1880509081 NY, 2004

Lourie B. and Smith R., *Slow Death By Rubber Duck*
Knopf Canada; Expanded, Updated Edition (January 15,
2019) ISBN-13 : 978-0735275706

ToxInToxOut, St Marys, NY, 2013, ISBN978-1-250-
05133-2

Tabrizian, I, *How to Read a 21st Century Hair Analysis,* (2014)
and *Visual Textbook of Nutritional Medicine* (undated)
www.nutritionreviewservice.com.au

van der Schaar, P, *Clinical Metal Toxicology,* 14th ed,
International Board of Clinical Metal Toxicology, 2017
(private publication)

ABOUT THE AUTHOR

Jon Gamble is trained in osteopathy, naturopathy and homeopathy and has practised Complementary Medicine since 1987. During this time, the prevalence of Chronic Fatigue Syndrome has rapidly increased, leading Jon to focus on the clinical understanding of the differing presentations of this condition. He has been able to develop unique ways of successfully treating associated obstinate and distressing gut disorders, using his personally developed combinations of diagnostic methods and treatment protocols.

He is the author of three practitioner books:

- *Accurate Daily Prescribing for a Successful Practice*
- *The Treatment of Irritable Bowel Syndrome*
- *Obstacles to Cure: Toxicity, Deficiency and Infection*

He has also co-authored *Treat Your Child Yourself; A parents guide to Drug Free Solutions for Common Complaints,* with his wife Nyema Hermiston, Registered Nurse, homeopath and naturopath.

Jon's specialty areas of treatment are:

- Allergies
- Chronic Fatigue Syndrome
- Digestive diseases
- Paediatrics.

Jon is an accredited practitioner with:

- Australian Register of Homeopaths (AROH)
- Australian Homeopathic Association (AHA)
- Australian Traditional-Medicine Society (ATMS)

Qualifications

- Bachelor of Arts (Monash University)
- Diploma of Naturopathy (British College of Naturopathy)
- Advanced Diploma of Homeopathy (Sydney College of Homeopathic Medicine)

Website: www.karunahealthcare.com.au

Email: jon@karunahealthcare.com.au